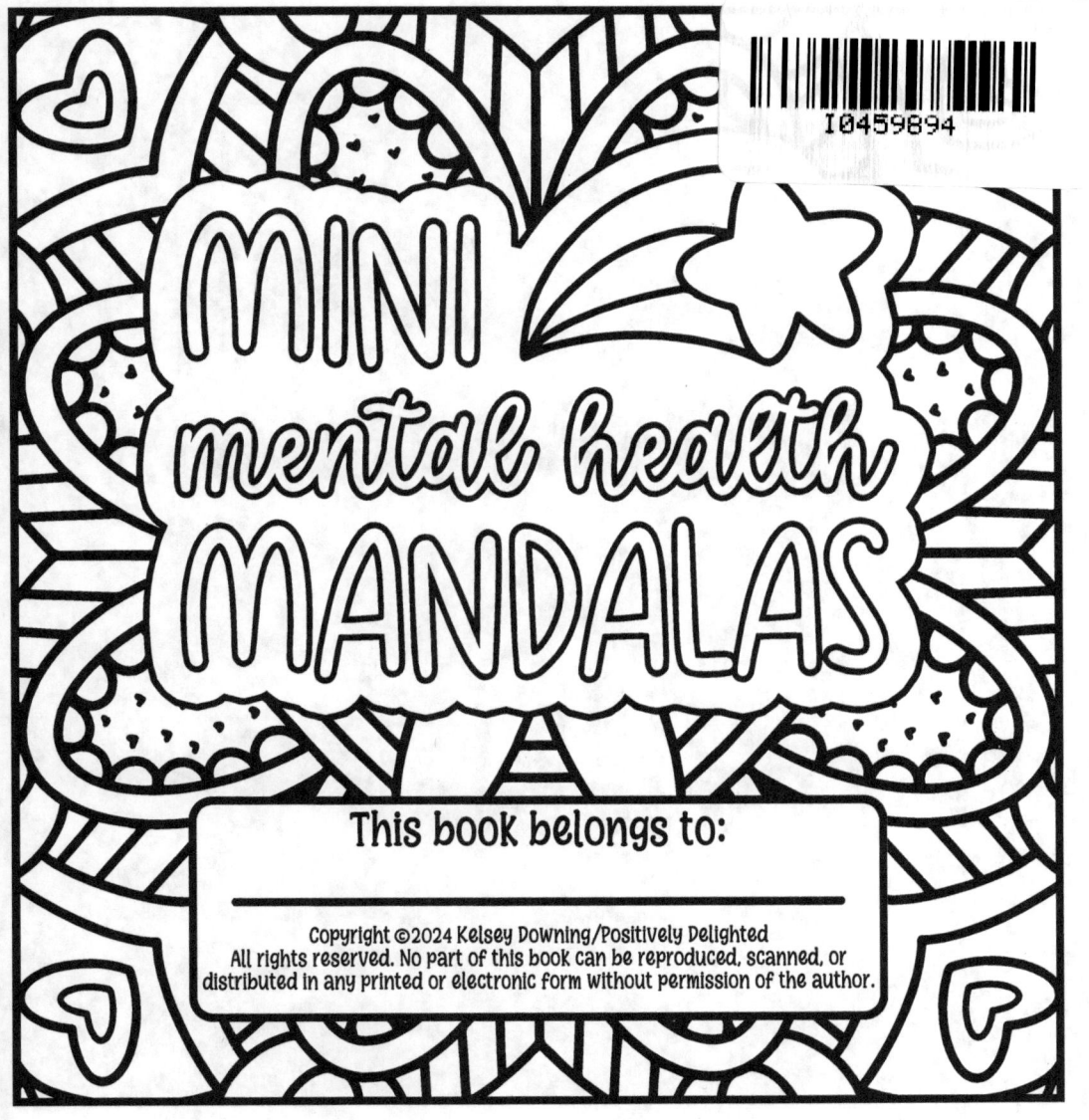

MINI
mental health
MANDALAS

This book belongs to:

_____

Color Testing Page

Use this page to test your crayons, colored pencils, markers, gel pens, & more!

Blotter Page

If using markers, cut out this page & put it behind your coloring page to prevent bleed.

INHALE CONFIDENCE EXHALE DOUBT

EVEN A BAD day is just 24 hours

DO YOUR BEST LET GO OF THE REST

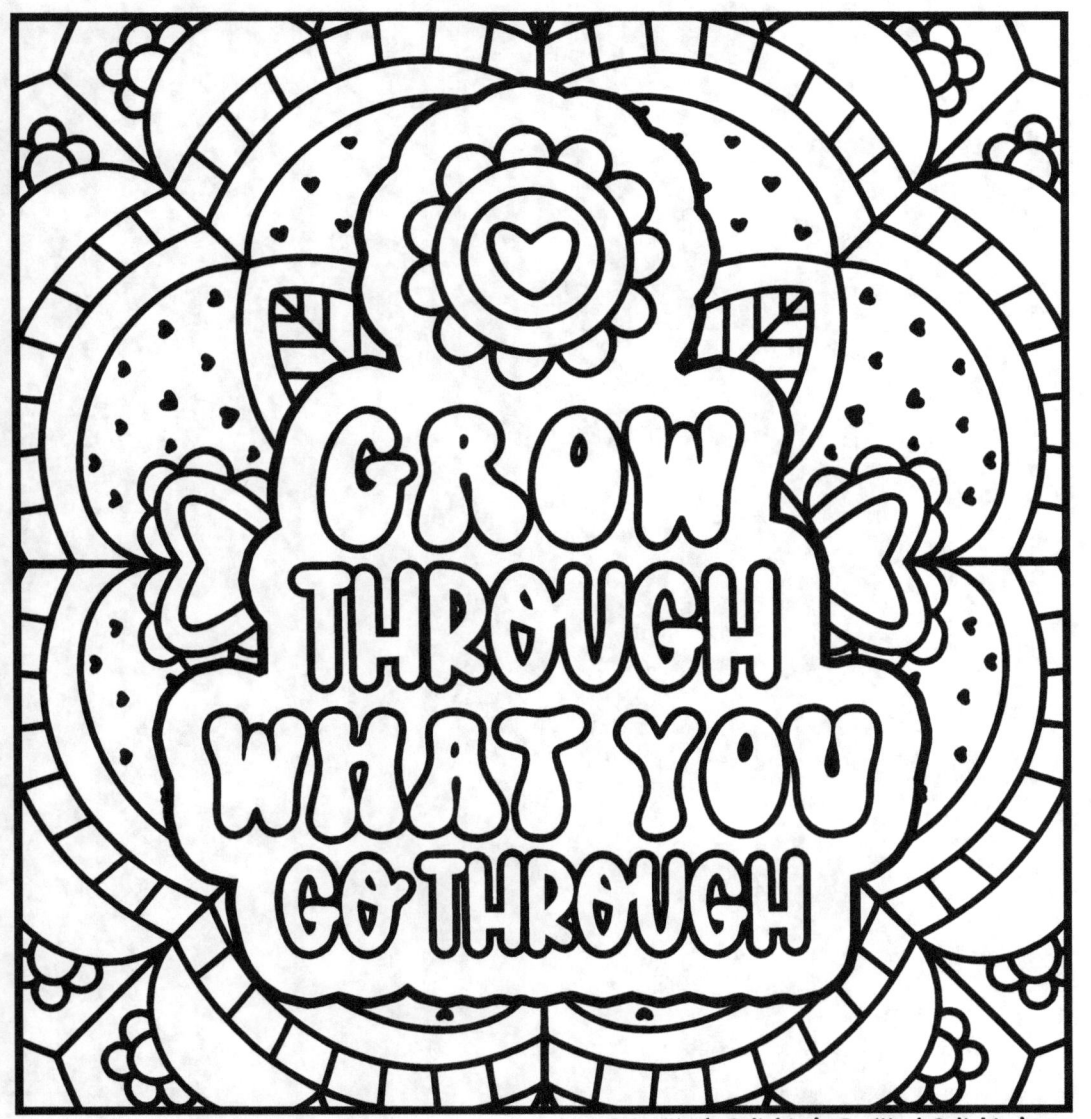

LET GO OF WHAT YOU can't change

EVERYTHING will be OKAY

IT'S OKAY TO CRY

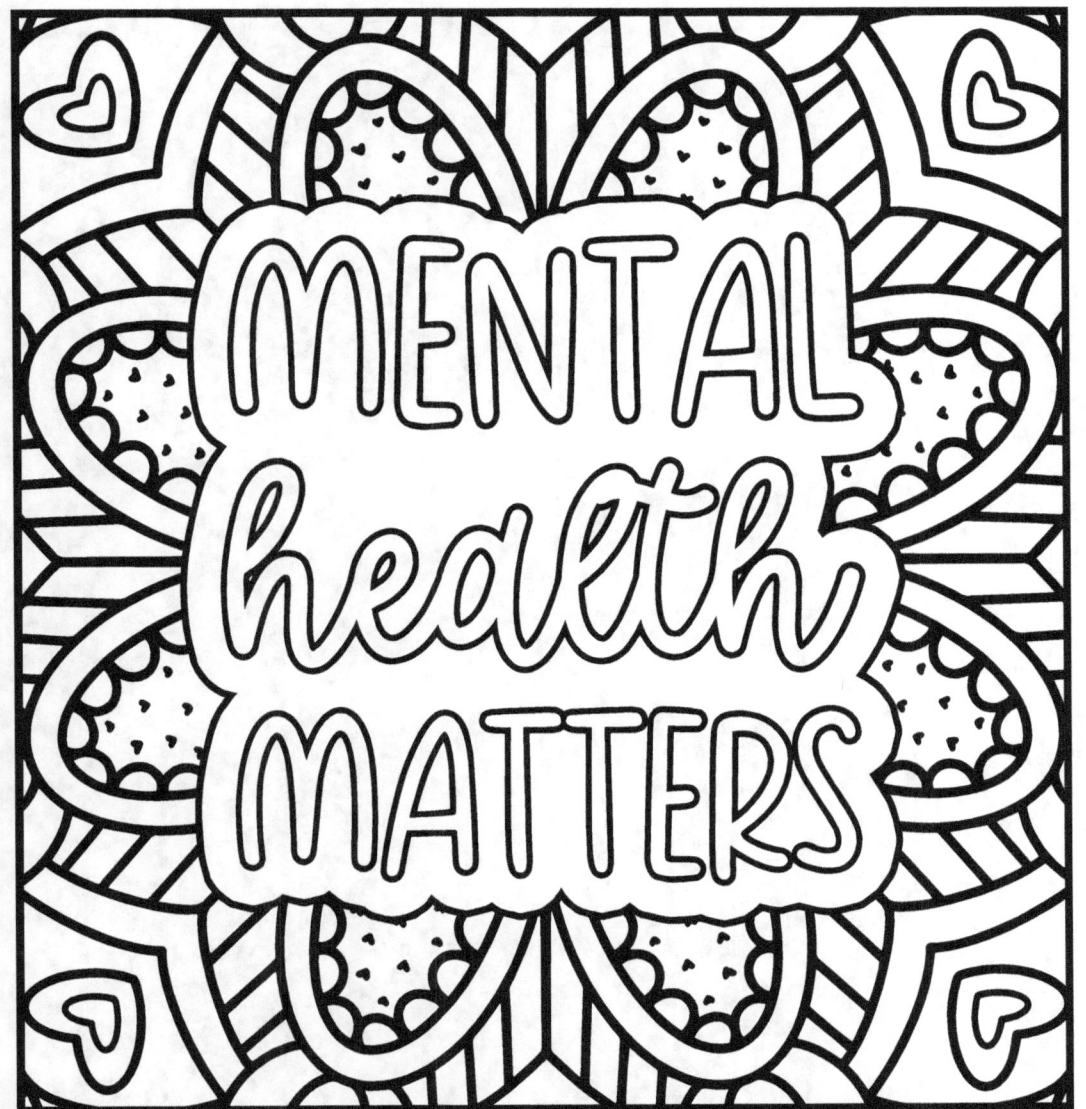

MENTAL health MATTERS

STARS CAN'T shine without DARKNESS

IT IS enough TO DO MY best

TODAY MY GOAL IS TO BE HAPPY NOT PERFECT

YOU ARE enough